Did You Enjoy Our Coloring Book?

We Want To Hear About It!

Help spread the word about our coloring books! The best way to spread the word is through reviews. We know how busy you are, especially with all of that coloring, but we would appreciate it!

Visit our website at www.arttherapycoloring.com

Over 200 Art Therapy Coloring Books

See our collection of over 200 Art Therapy Coloring Books for Adults, Men, Women, Seniors, Teens, Kids, Boys, and Girls.

Coloring Books For Girls

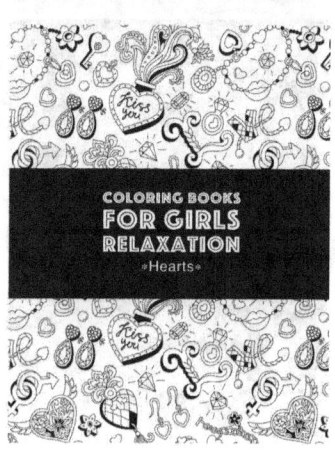

Art Therapy Coloring Books

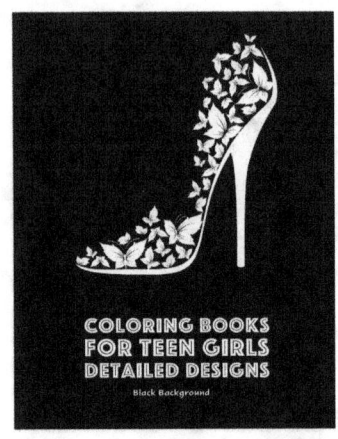

COLORING BOOKS
FOR TEEN GIRLS
DETAILED DESIGNS
Black Background

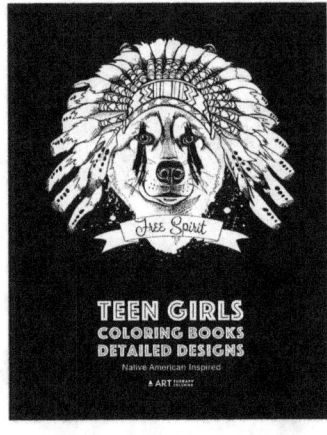

TEEN GIRLS
COLORING BOOKS
DETAILED DESIGNS
Native American Inspired

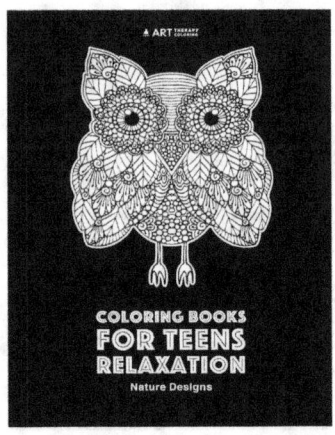

COLORING BOOKS
FOR TEENS
RELAXATION
Nature Designs

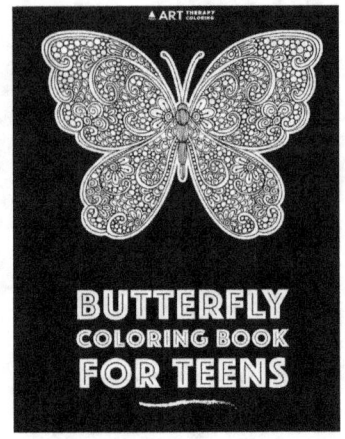

BUTTERFLY
COLORING BOOK
FOR TEENS

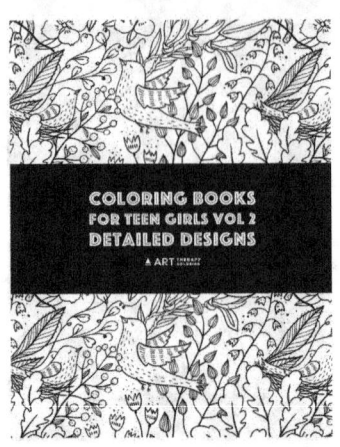

COLORING BOOKS
FOR TEEN GIRLS VOL 2
DETAILED DESIGNS

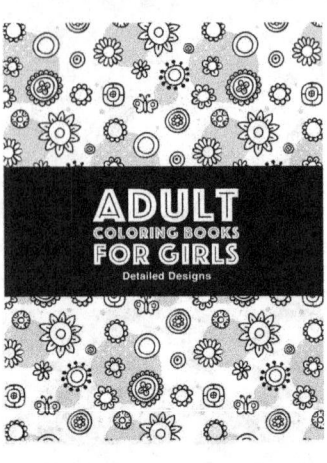

ADULT
COLORING BOOKS
FOR GIRLS
Detailed Designs

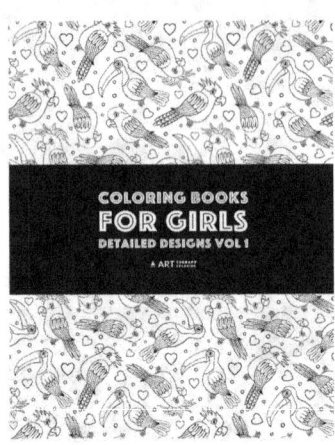

COLORING BOOKS
FOR GIRLS
DETAILED DESIGNS VOL 1

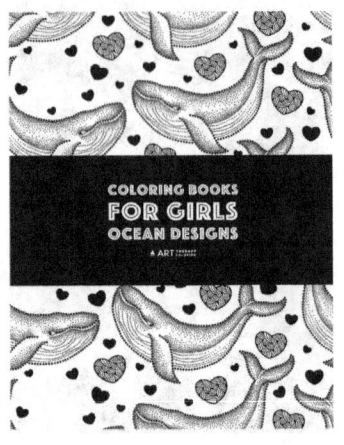

COLORING BOOKS
FOR GIRLS
OCEAN DESIGNS

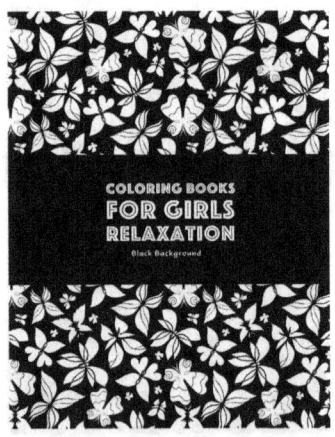

COLORING BOOKS
FOR GIRLS
RELAXATION
Black Background

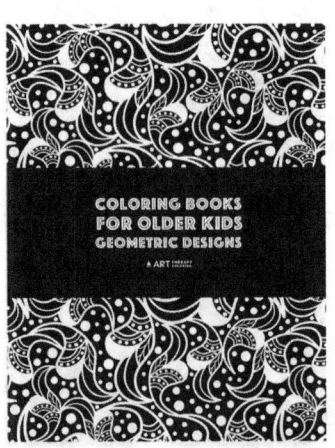

COLORING BOOKS
FOR OLDER KIDS
GEOMETRIC DESIGNS

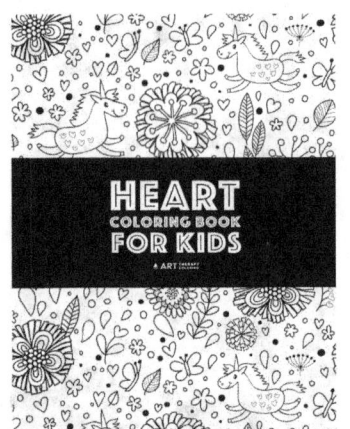

HEART
COLORING BOOK
FOR KIDS

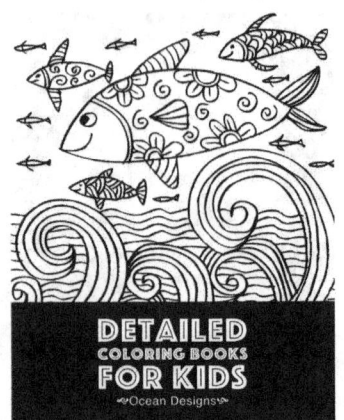

DETAILED
COLORING BOOKS
FOR KIDS
Ocean Designs

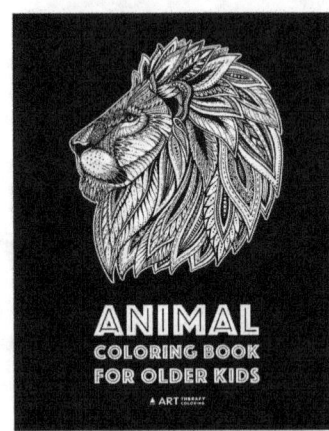

ANIMAL
COLORING BOOK
FOR OLDER KIDS

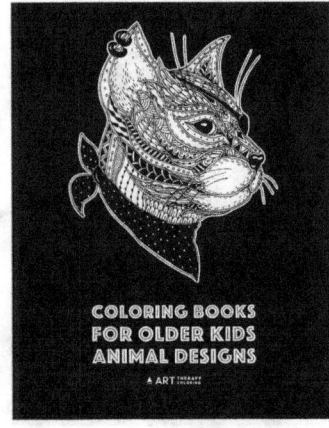

COLORING BOOKS
FOR OLDER KIDS
ANIMAL DESIGNS

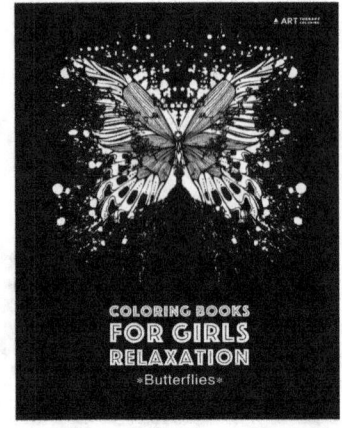

COLORING BOOKS
FOR GIRLS
RELAXATION
Butterflies

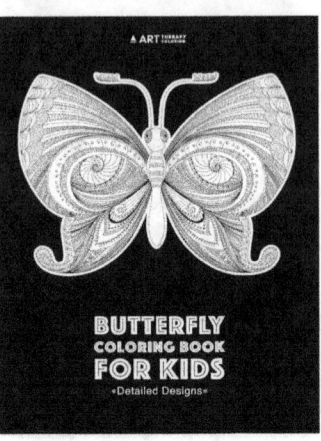

BUTTERFLY
COLORING BOOK
FOR KIDS
Detailed Designs

Coloring Books For Kids

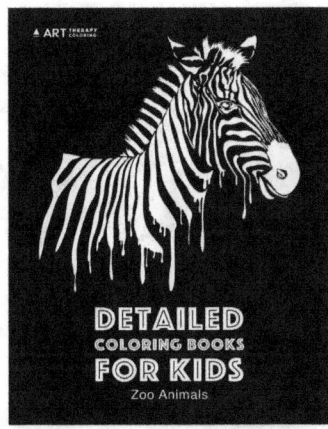

DETAILED
COLORING BOOKS
FOR KIDS
Zoo Animals

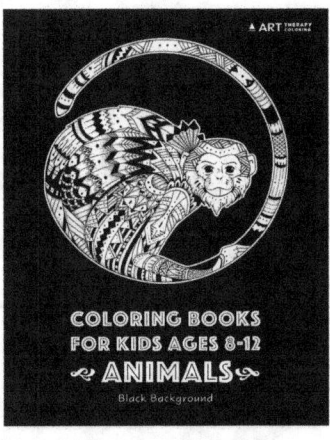

COLORING BOOKS
FOR KIDS AGES 8-12
~ANIMALS~
Black Background

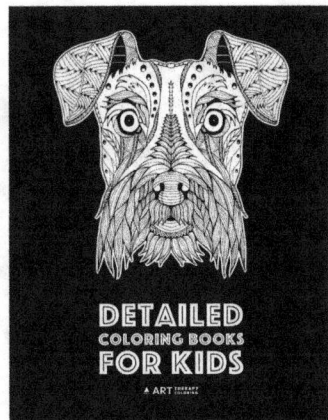

DETAILED
COLORING BOOKS
FOR KIDS

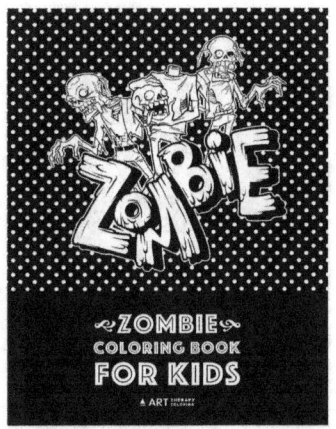

~ZOMBIE~
COLORING BOOK
FOR KIDS

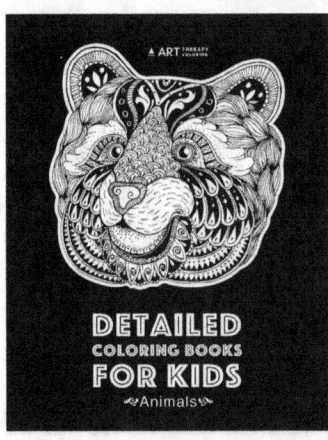

DETAILED
COLORING BOOKS
FOR KIDS
~Animals~

DETAILED
COLORING BOOKS
FOR KIDS
~Elephants~

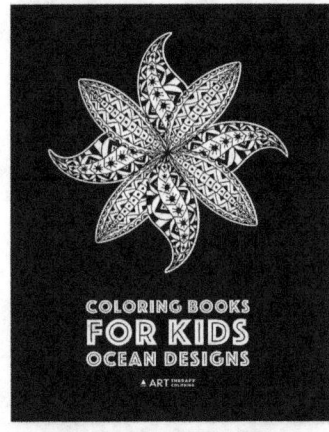

COLORING BOOKS
FOR KIDS
OCEAN DESIGNS

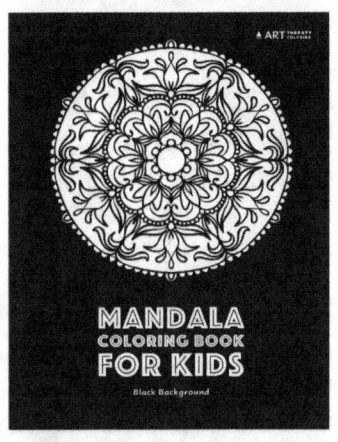

MANDALA
COLORING BOOK
FOR KIDS
Black Background

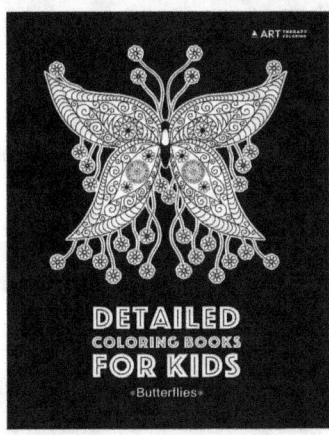

DETAILED
COLORING BOOKS
FOR KIDS
~Butterflies~

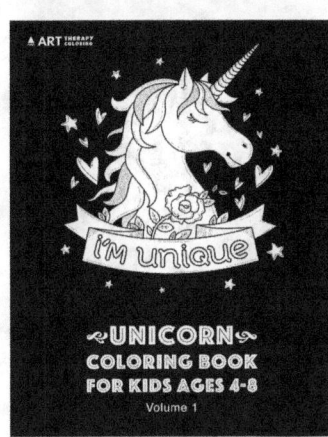

~UNICORN~
COLORING BOOK
FOR KIDS AGES 4-8
Volume 1

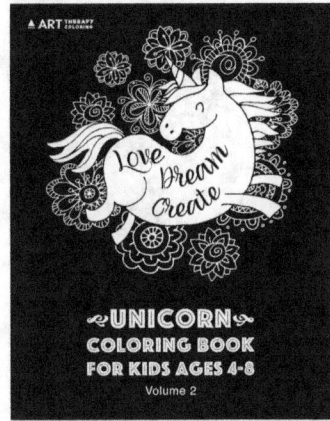

~UNICORN~
COLORING BOOK
FOR KIDS AGES 4-8
Volume 2

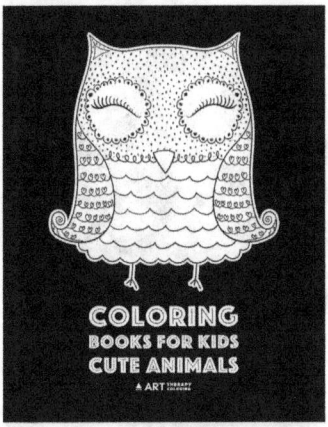

COLORING
BOOKS FOR KIDS
CUTE ANIMALS

~KIDS~
MANDALA
COLORING BOOK

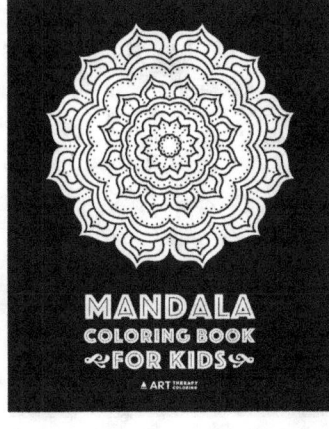

MANDALA
COLORING BOOK
FOR KIDS

~SHARK~
COLORING BOOK

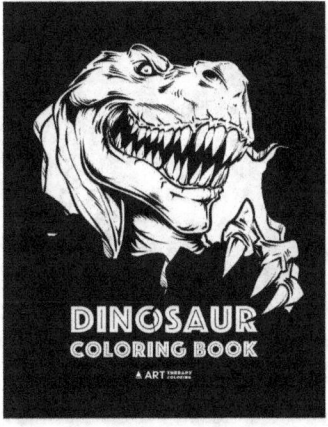

DINOSAUR
COLORING BOOK

Coloring Books For Boys

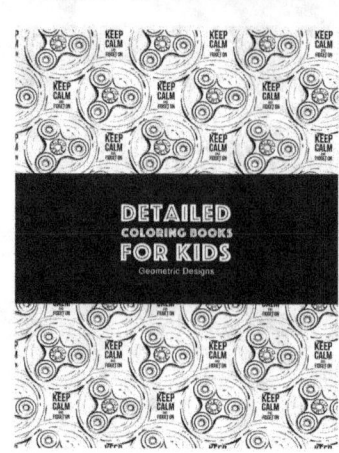

Coloring Books For Teens

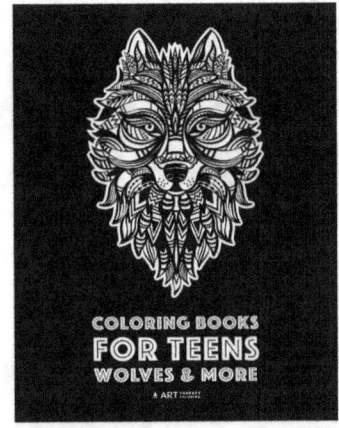

COLORING BOOKS
FOR TEENS
WOLVES & MORE

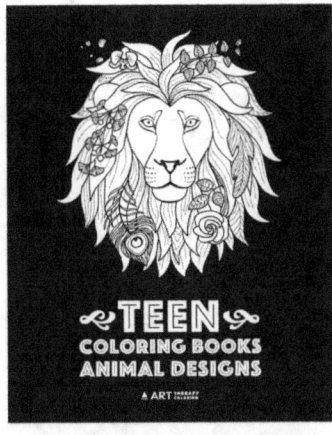

TEEN
COLORING BOOKS
ANIMAL DESIGNS

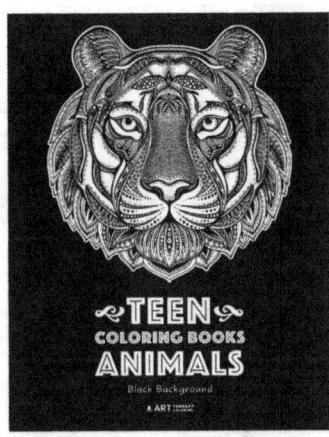

TEEN
COLORING BOOKS
ANIMALS
Black Background

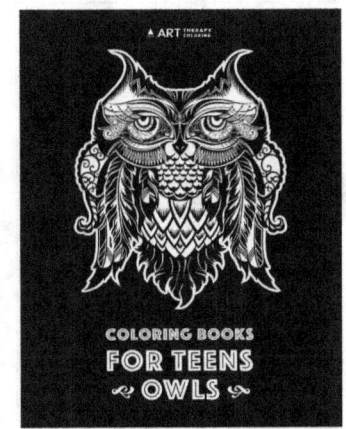

COLORING BOOKS
FOR TEENS
OWLS

TEEN
INSPIRATIONAL
COLORING BOOKS

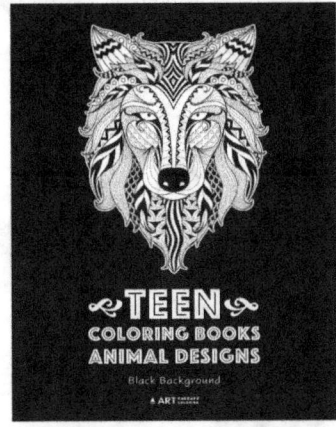

TEEN
COLORING BOOKS
ANIMAL DESIGNS
Black Background

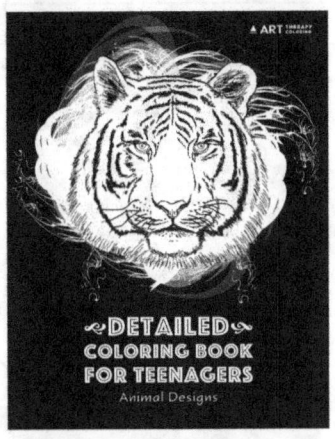

DETAILED
COLORING BOOK
FOR TEENAGERS
Animal Designs

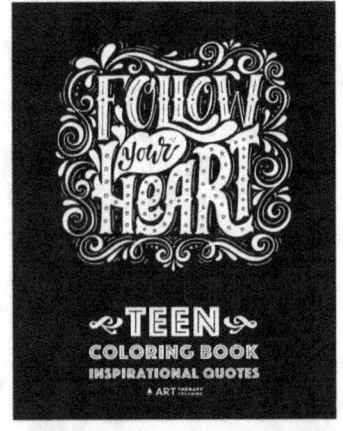

TEEN
COLORING BOOK
INSPIRATIONAL QUOTES

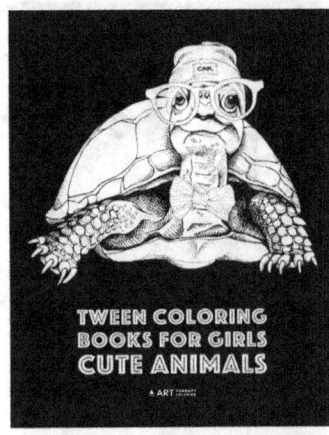

TWEEN COLORING
BOOKS FOR GIRLS
CUTE ANIMALS

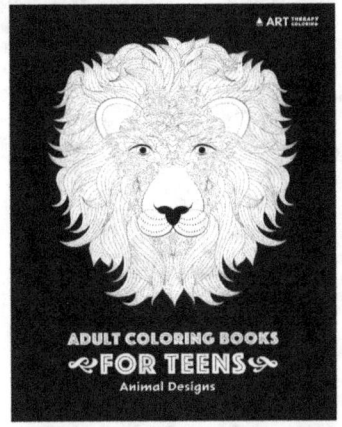

ADULT COLORING BOOKS
FOR TEENS
Animal Designs

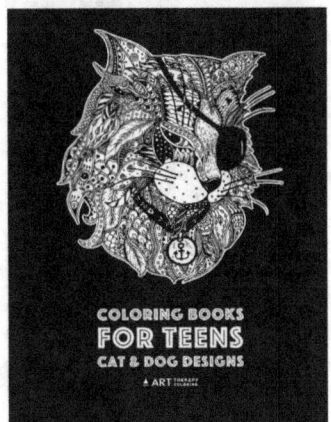

COLORING BOOKS
FOR TEENS
CAT & DOG DESIGNS

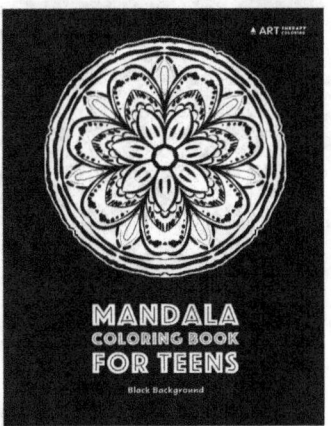

MANDALA
COLORING BOOK
FOR TEENS
Black Background

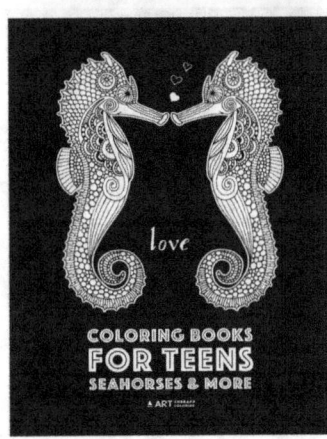

COLORING BOOKS
FOR TEENS
SEAHORSES & MORE

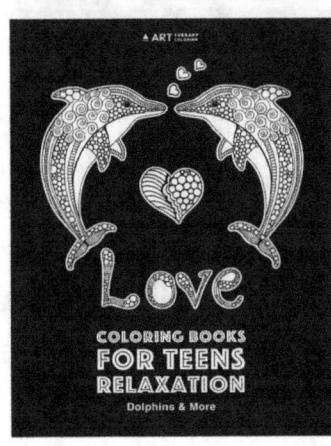

COLORING BOOKS
FOR TEENS
RELAXATION
Dolphins & More

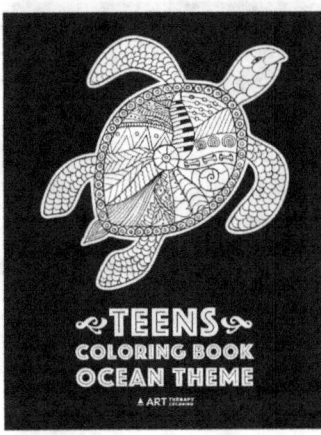

TEENS
COLORING BOOK
OCEAN THEME

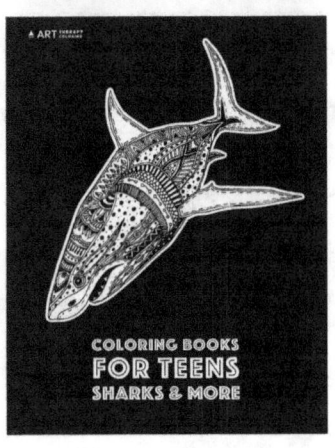

COLORING BOOKS
FOR TEENS
SHARKS & MORE

Coloring Books For Teens

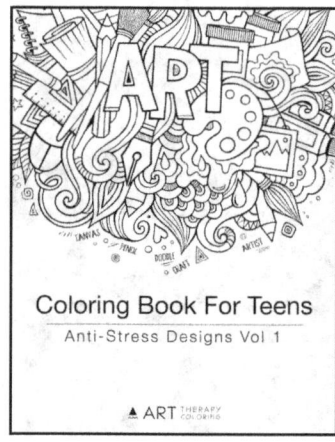

Coloring Book For Teens
Anti-Stress Designs Vol 1

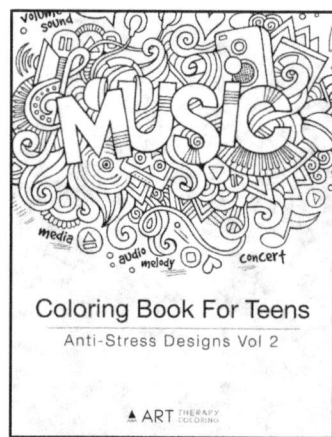

Coloring Book For Teens
Anti-Stress Designs Vol 2

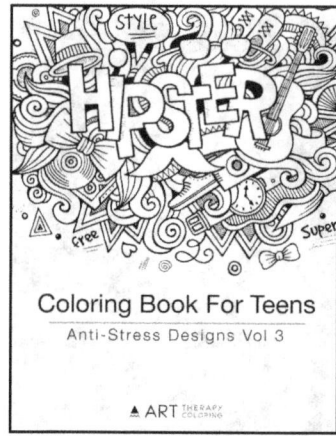

Coloring Book For Teens
Anti-Stress Designs Vol 3

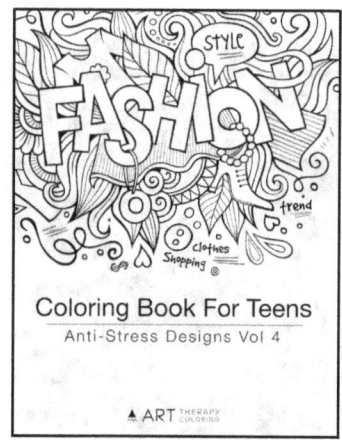

Coloring Book For Teens
Anti-Stress Designs Vol 4

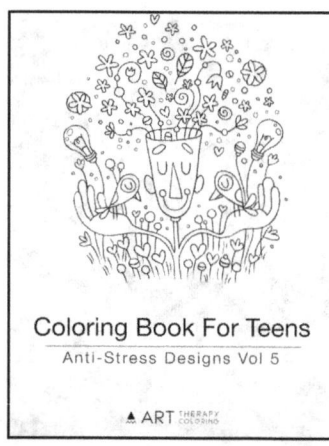

Coloring Book For Teens
Anti-Stress Designs Vol 5

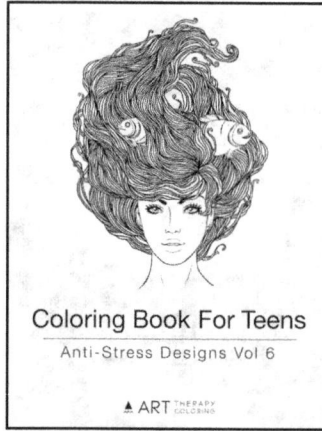

Coloring Book For Teens
Anti-Stress Designs Vol 6

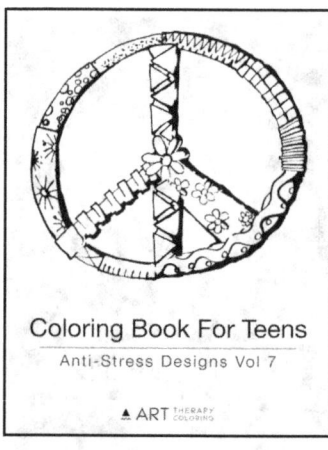

Coloring Book For Teens
Anti-Stress Designs Vol 7

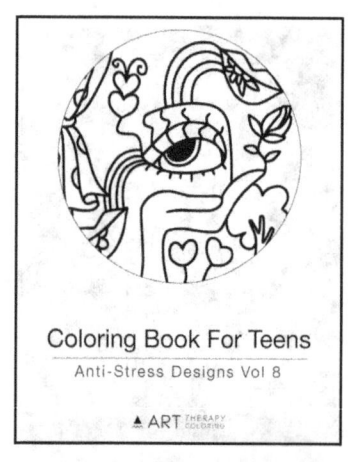

Coloring Book For Teens
Anti-Stress Designs Vol 8

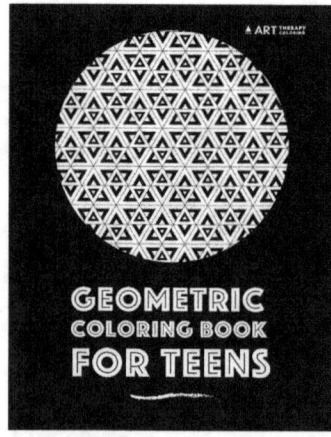

GEOMETRIC COLORING BOOK FOR TEENS

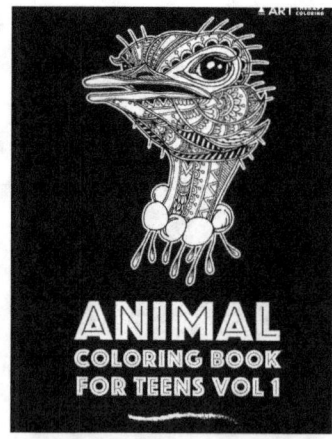

ANIMAL COLORING BOOK FOR TEENS VOL 1

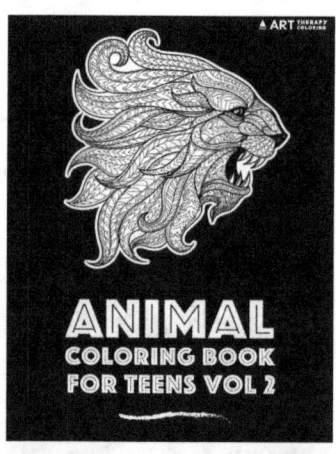

ANIMAL COLORING BOOK FOR TEENS VOL 2

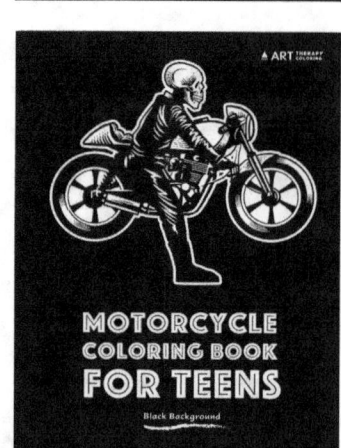

MOTORCYCLE COLORING BOOK FOR TEENS
Black Background

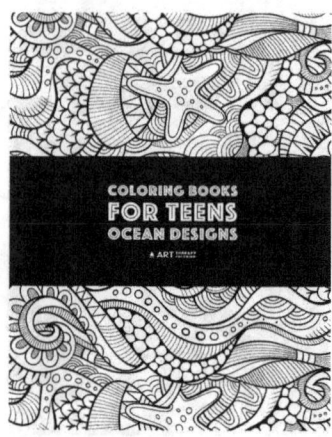

COLORING BOOKS FOR TEENS OCEAN DESIGNS

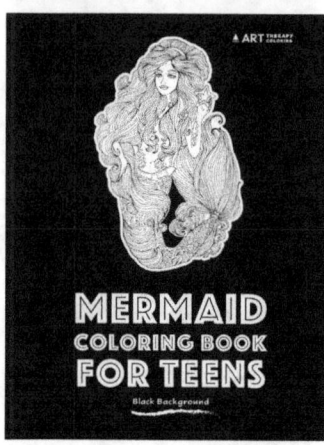

MERMAID COLORING BOOK FOR TEENS
Black Background

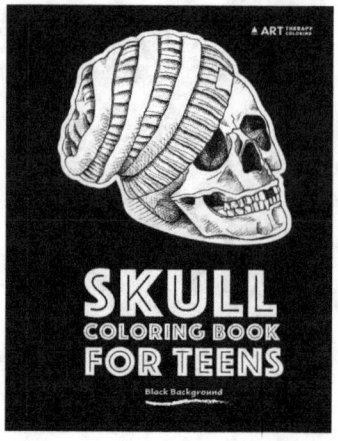

SKULL COLORING BOOK FOR TEENS
Black Background

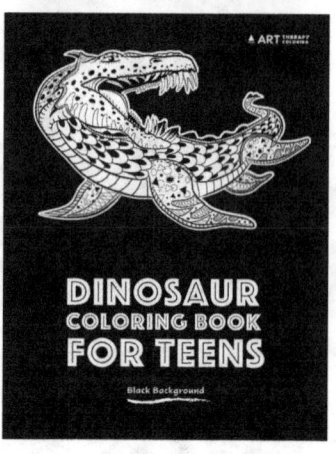

DINOSAUR COLORING BOOK FOR TEENS
Black Background

Coloring Books For Adults

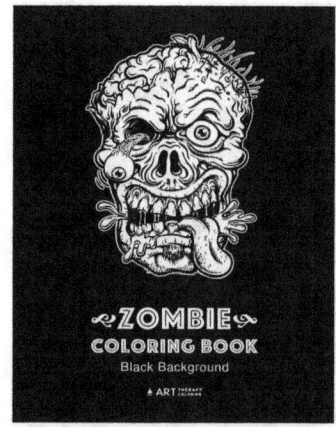

ZOMBIE
COLORING BOOK
Black Background

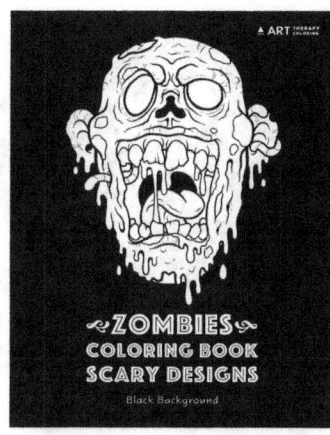

ZOMBIES
COLORING BOOK
SCARY DESIGNS
Black Background

DRAGON
COLORING BOOK

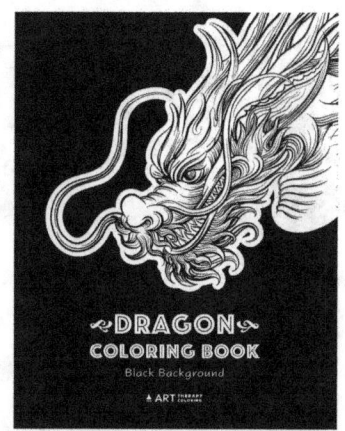

DRAGON
COLORING BOOK
Black Background

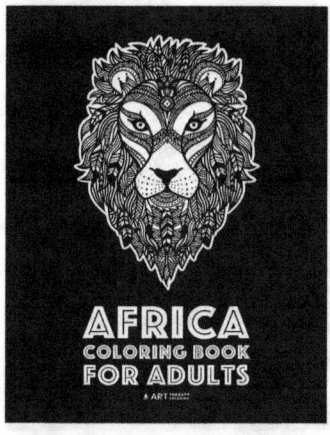

AFRICA
COLORING BOOK
FOR ADULTS

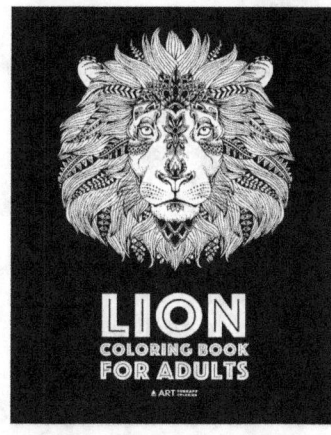

LION
COLORING BOOK
FOR ADULTS

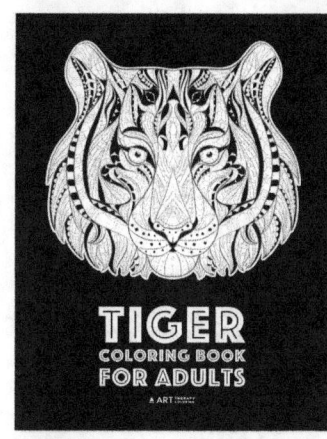

TIGER
COLORING BOOK
FOR ADULTS

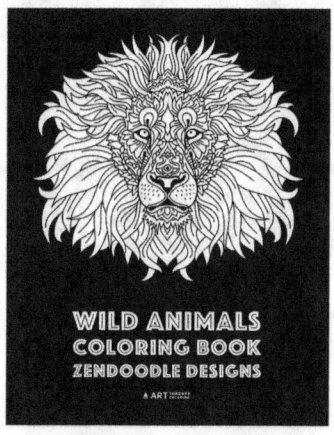

WILD ANIMALS
COLORING BOOK
ZENDOODLE DESIGNS

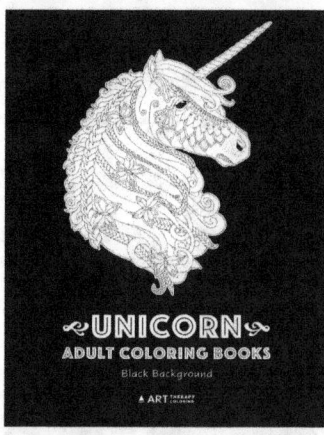

UNICORN
ADULT COLORING BOOKS
Black Background

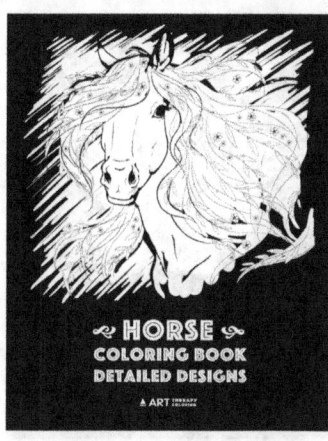

HORSE
COLORING BOOK
DETAILED DESIGNS

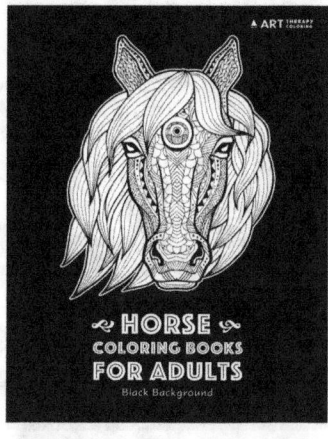

HORSE
COLORING BOOK
FOR ADULTS
Black Background

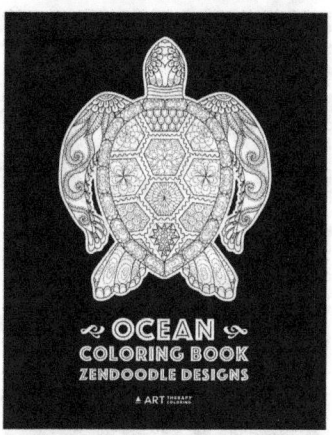

OCEAN
COLORING BOOK
ZENDOODLE DESIGNS

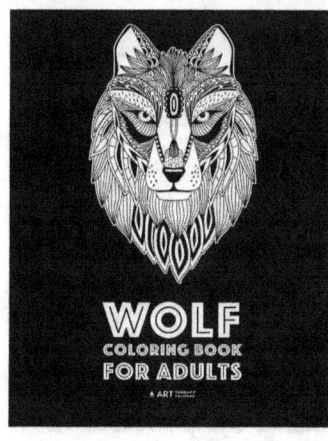

WOLF
COLORING BOOK
FOR ADULTS

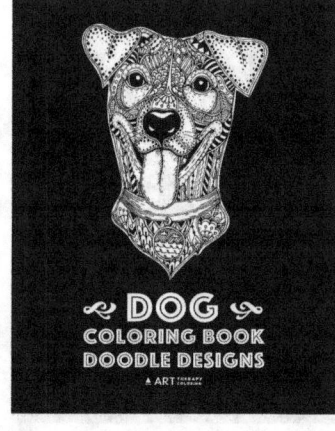

DOG
COLORING BOOK
DOODLE DESIGNS

CUTE ANIMAL
COLORING BOOK

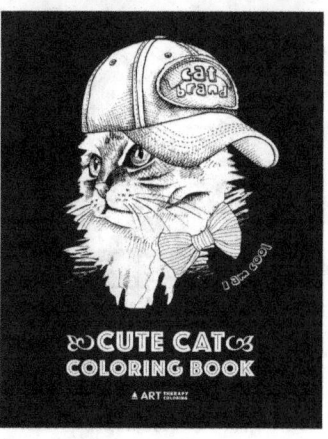

CUTE CAT
COLORING BOOK

Coloring Books For Adults

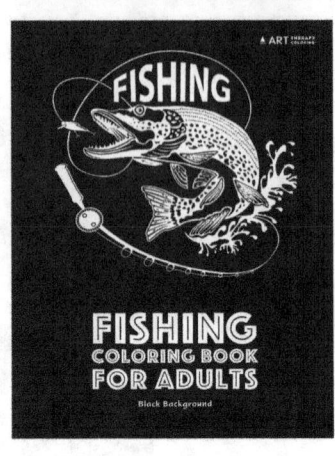

Coloring Books For Adults

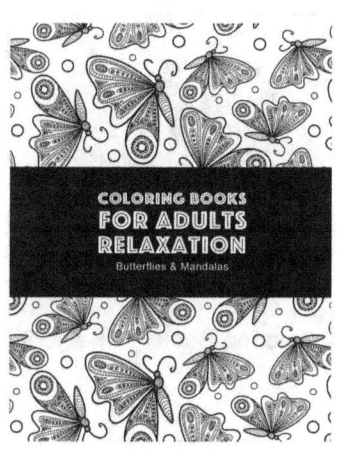

Coloring Books For Seniors

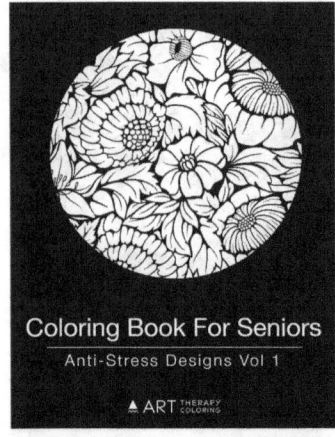

Coloring Book For Seniors
Anti-Stress Designs Vol 1

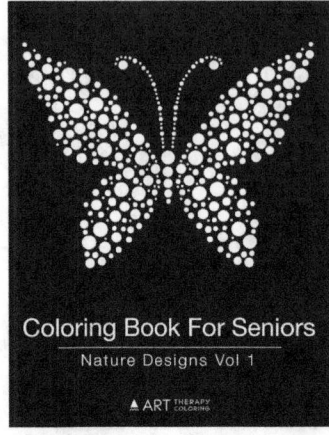

Coloring Book For Seniors
Nature Designs Vol 1

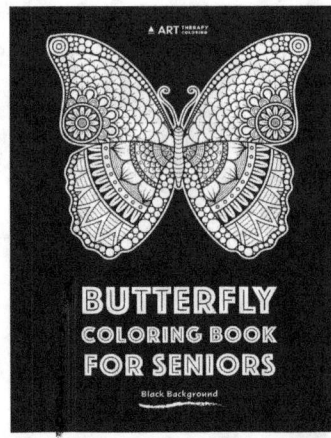

BUTTERFLY COLORING BOOK FOR SENIORS
Black Background

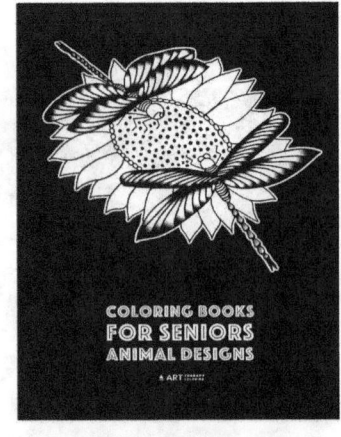

COLORING BOOKS FOR SENIORS ANIMAL DESIGNS

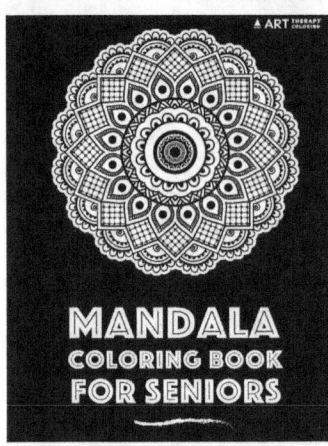

MANDALA COLORING BOOK FOR SENIORS

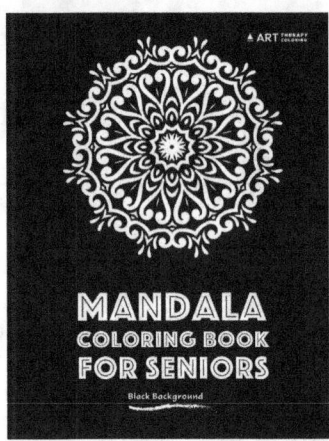

MANDALA COLORING BOOK FOR SENIORS
Black Background

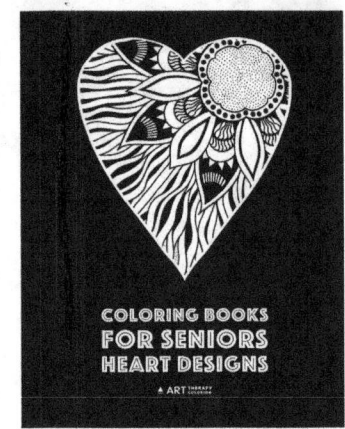

COLORING BOOKS FOR SENIORS HEART DESIGNS

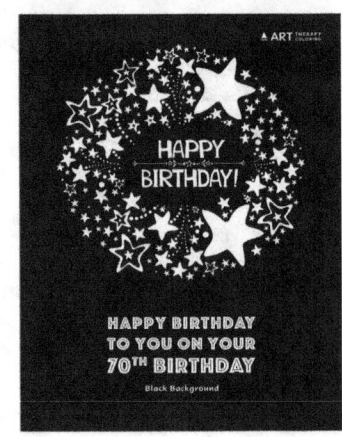

HAPPY BIRTHDAY TO YOU ON YOUR 70TH BIRTHDAY
Black Background

COLORING BOOKS FOR SENIORS SWIRL DESIGNS
Black Background

COLORING BOOKS FOR SENIORS RELAXING DESIGNS

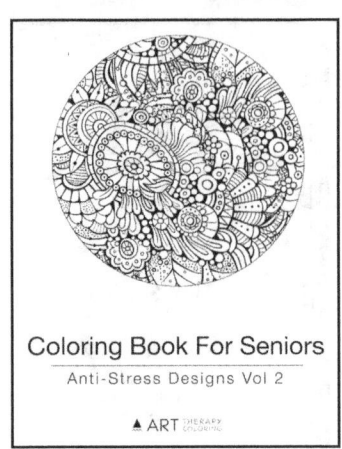

Coloring Book For Seniors
Anti-Stress Designs Vol 2

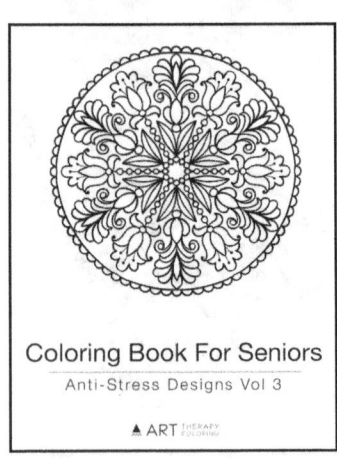

Coloring Book For Seniors
Anti-Stress Designs Vol 3

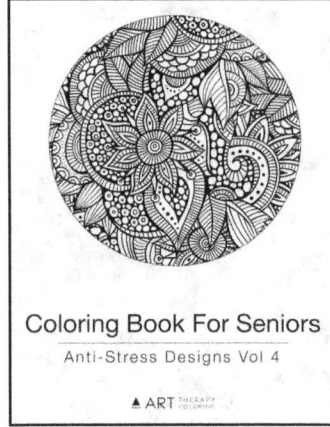

Coloring Book For Seniors
Anti-Stress Designs Vol 4

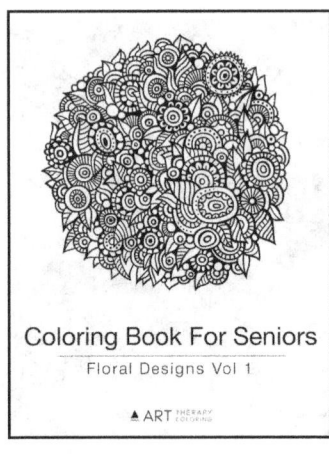

Coloring Book For Seniors
Floral Designs Vol 1

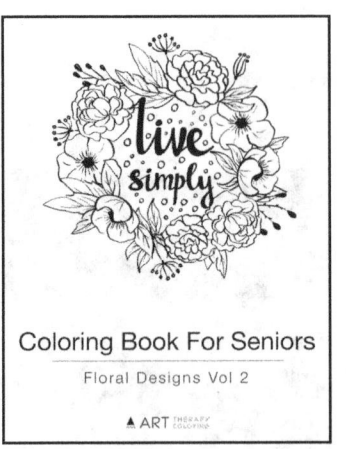

Coloring Book For Seniors
Floral Designs Vol 2

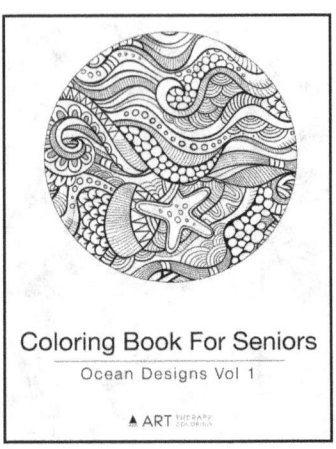

Coloring Book For Seniors
Ocean Designs Vol 1

Coloring Books For Men

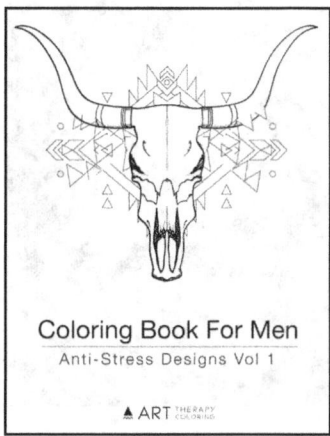

Coloring Book For Men
Anti-Stress Designs Vol 1
ART THERAPY COLORING

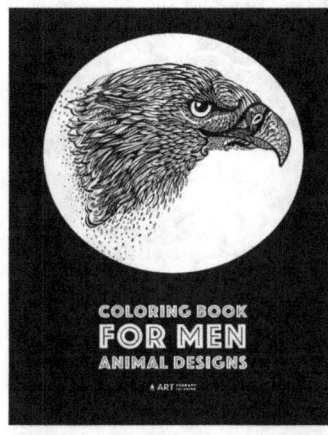

COLORING BOOK FOR MEN
ANIMAL DESIGNS

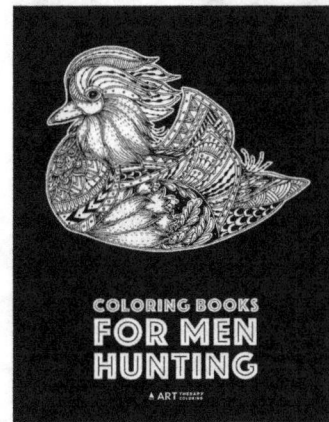

COLORING BOOKS FOR MEN
HUNTING

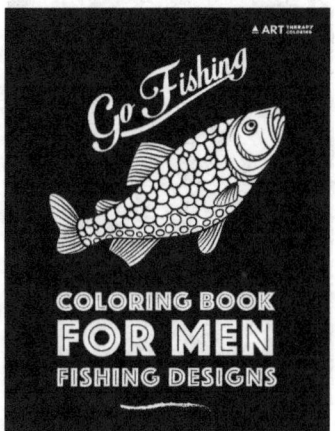

Go Fishing
COLORING BOOK FOR MEN
FISHING DESIGNS

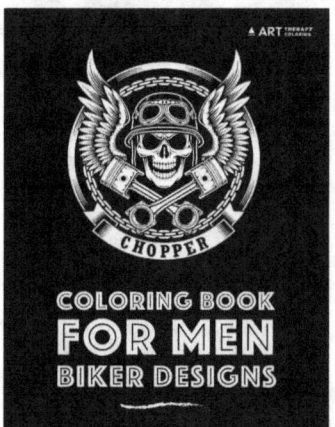

CHOPPER
COLORING BOOK FOR MEN
BIKER DESIGNS

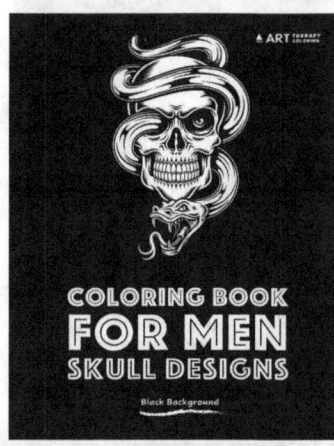

COLORING BOOK FOR MEN
SKULL DESIGNS
Black Background

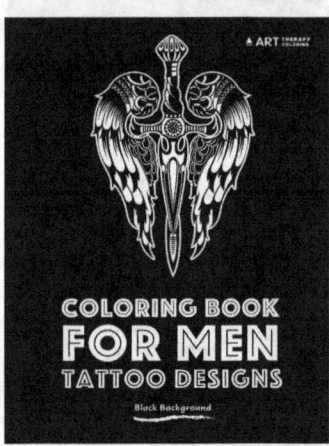

COLORING BOOK FOR MEN
TATTOO DESIGNS
Black Background

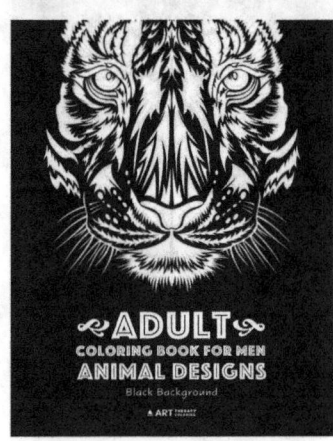

ADULT
COLORING BOOK FOR MEN
ANIMAL DESIGNS
Black Background

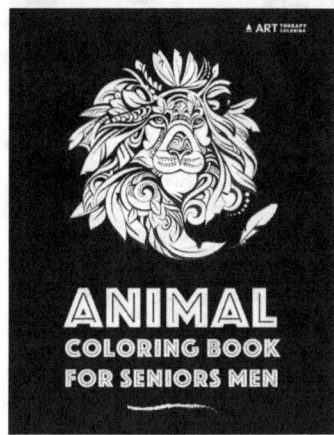

ANIMAL
COLORING BOOK
FOR SENIORS MEN

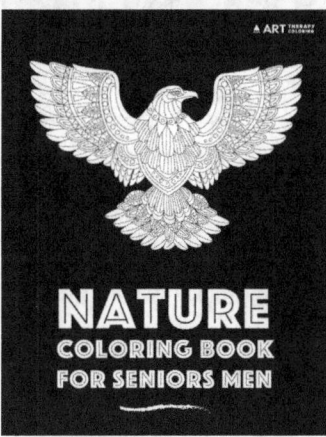

NATURE
COLORING BOOK
FOR SENIORS MEN

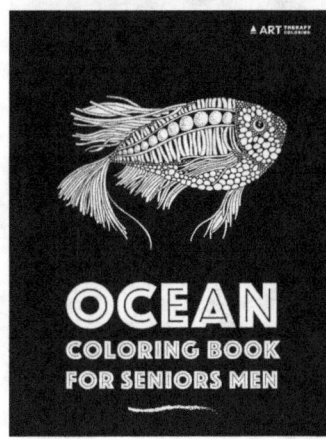

OCEAN
COLORING BOOK
FOR SENIORS MEN

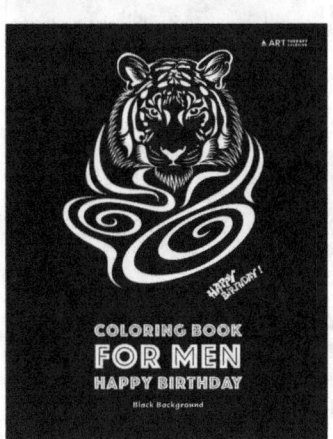

COLORING BOOK FOR MEN
HAPPY BIRTHDAY
Black Background

Coloring Books For Special Occasions

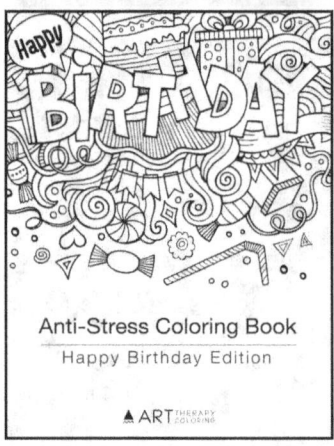

Coloring Books For Teen Girls Vol 2
Detailed Designs

Published by:
Art Therapy Coloring
El Dorado Hills, California
www.arttherapycoloring.com

Shutterstock Images

ISBN: 978-1-64126-039-8